published&black™
MAGAZINE

NEW RELEASE

IN SUPPORT OF BREAST CANCER MONTH

2022 DAILY GOAL PLANNER

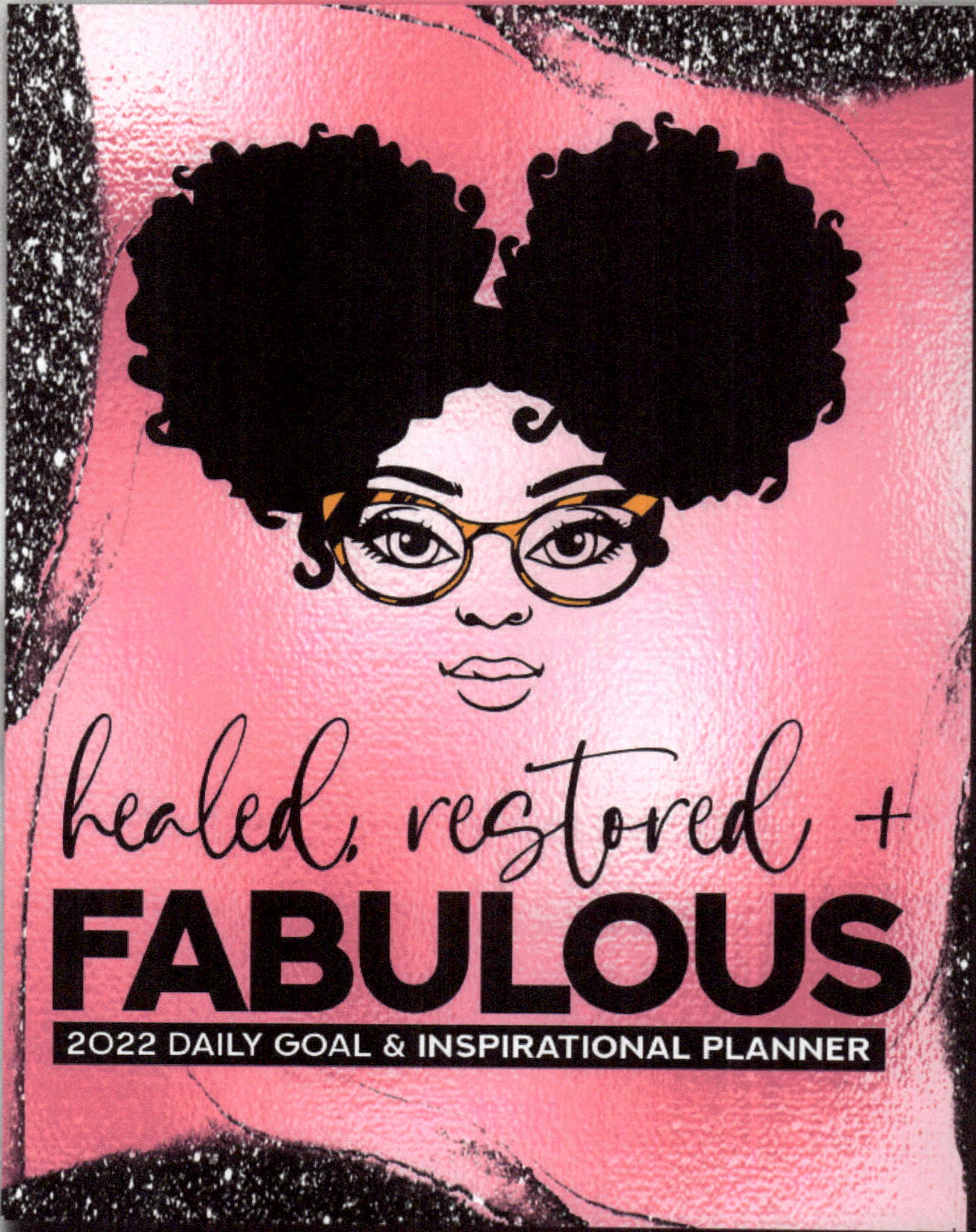

AVAILABLE NOW ON AMAZON

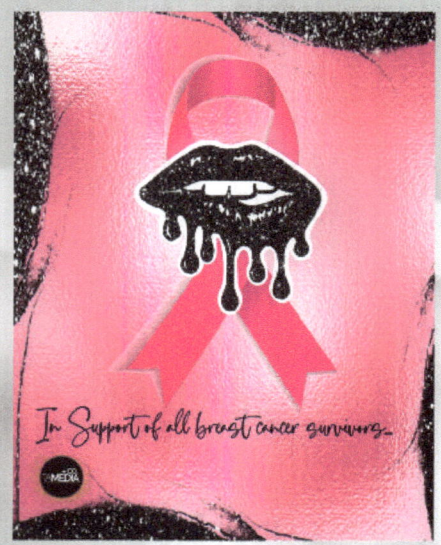

EDITOR-IN-CHIEF + PUBLISHER

TIFFANY A. GREEN-HOOD

CREATOR of **BLACK WRITER SPACE**

Greetings, to my readers. Finally making it to this place I'll say is one of my greatest accomplishments in life. I can still remember my mother telling me how I was always writing even at the early age of three. It's always been a dream of mine to provide a platform for writers and authors to be able to come and get the resources and answers they need to be successful in publsihing.

As I bring to you, Published & Black Magazine, I promise to bring fire content to push black indendent authors into their next level. We are no longer aspiring to be authors we are living in it. Becoming a NYT Bestseller was the goal back in the day. Now we are walking in our author CEO positions. Thats it, thats all. Author branding brings us the certifications we need to excel and build with. Who has time to wait for book sales? We are now building author empires if I may say so. The book must be the platform we learn to build from not to depend on and wait for a book deal. We count our own coins, call our own shots and build complte wealth in our own businesses. With that being said, I bring to you this magazine to celebrate, highlight and build credibility and educate indenpendent black authors.

> "I PROMISE TO BRING FIRE CONTENT TO PUSH AUTHORS TO THEIR NEXT LEVEL."

CEO ~ *Tiffany A. Green-Hood*

published**&black**™

Contents

Introduction

4 Editor-in-Chief

8 Ayanna Bean
The debut of her new book and her story of how she triumphed through the imposible

12 Ayanna Mills-Ambrose

16 Favorite Places to Write

18 Dawn Francis

22 Jenise McNair

26 Publishing Secrets

28 Mario Givens

32 Covid + **Book Sales**

34 Mikayla Diamond

42 **Tiffany A Green-Hood**

WE PRESENT TO YOU THE

published&black
MAGAZINE

25 TOP BLACK AUTHORS OF 2021

We've seen her on **BET's American Gangster Trap Queens** series telling her story to the world. In episode 7 Ayana broke down simply how she stole over 300K in finanacial aid to fund her record label.

Yes. she did the crime she and did her time. So what's next? What we don't know is, Ayana has so much in store for her future. She has no time to stay stangnant at what she did, how and why. At the end of the day Ayana knows she was created for success.

In her new book, **"A Year And A Day"** she breaks down the chapters of her life before American Gangster Trap Queens was even a thing. Who was she when no one knew her? Everyone has a backstory and she is ready to release hers.

Like she says with so much power in her episode, **"She was addicted to not being broke"**. Fast forward, 2021, Ayana is looking forward to growing and continuing to build a legacy for her life, her children, family and those who support her.

Published & Black Magazine had the pleasure of chatting with Ms. Bean about her plans for her future as a **CEO**.

"ADDICTED TO NOT BEING BROKE"

CEO~Ayana Bean

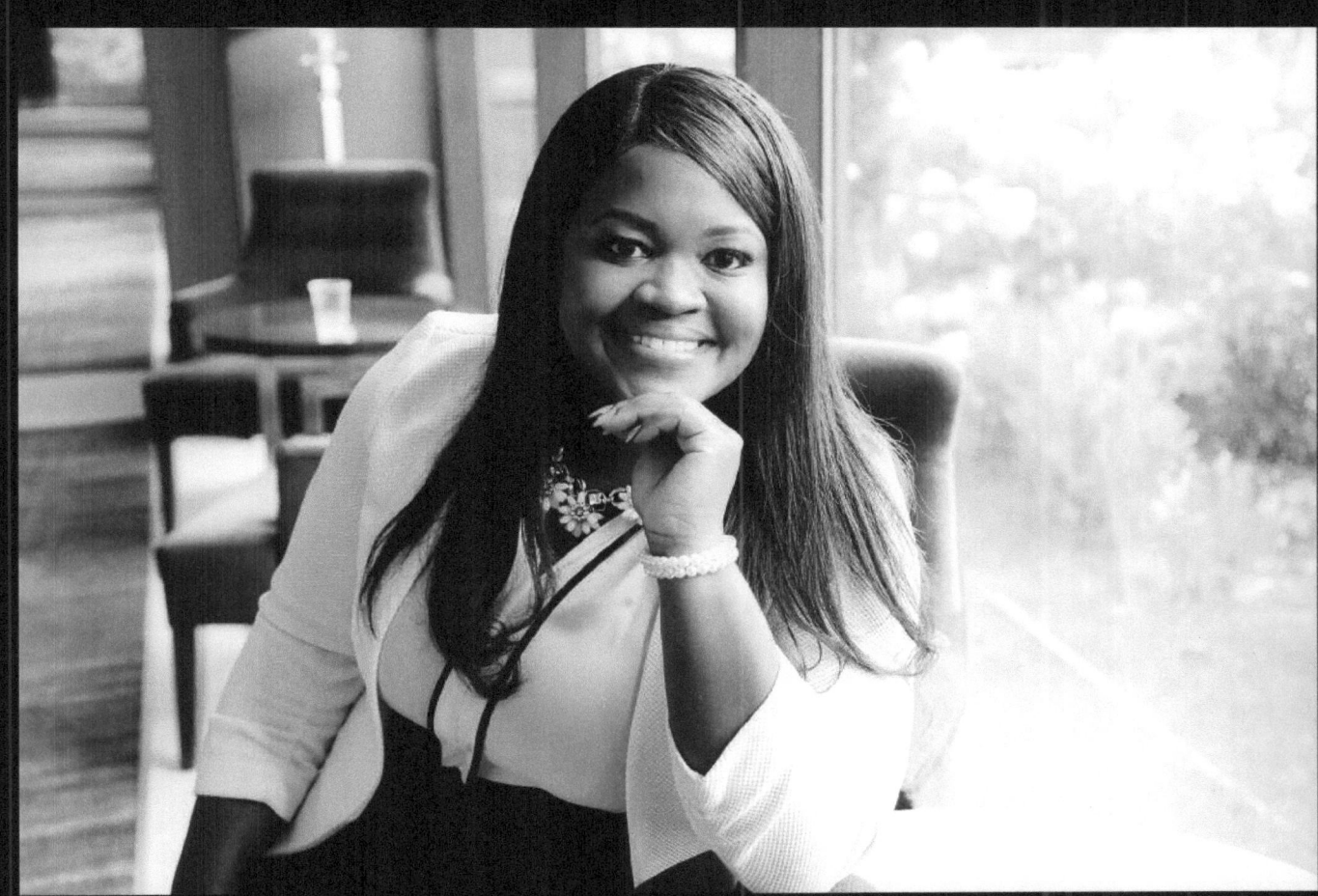

author.

AYANNA MILLS-AMBROSE

BEST-SELLING AUTHOR BOOK COACH
AND LITERARY MARKETING MOGUL

Ayanna Mills Ambrose (Gallow), M.B.A., is a Literary Strategist that maximizes success. She entered the literary world as an author of the Amazon International Best- Selling Book, God & Hip Hop, A 21 Day Biblical Devotional Inspired by Hip Hop. Since God & Hip Hop's debut, she has become the Amazon bestselling author of 18 other books and a Licensed & Ordained Evangelist. Ayanna is also the creator of the Write Pray Release book and program designed to equip the masses to self-reflect on past hurt, write it out, and release the pain. Ayanna empowers women to embrace their past stories of triumph and tragedy as the core of their success. She is the creator of God & Hip Hop...a proprietary system that has produced 46 cohort Amazon International Best-Selling Authors. Writers who, like her, were once afraid to share their stories due to shame. Through her company, Thanx A Mills, LLC,

Ayanna has delivered numerous literary and empowerment speeches and helped over 150 authors to achieve their Best-Selling dreams through marketing and publishing. Her work is rooted in seeing the power in turning what was designed to destroy you into something that propels you. Ayanna is a native of New York but a current resident of Georgia. She is a happy wife and mom to three sons. She can breached at the below.

Ayanna Mills Ambrose (Gallow), M.B.A., is a Literary Strategist that maximizes success.

She entered the literary world as an author of the Amazon International Best- Selling Book, God & Hip Hop, A 21 Day Biblical Devotional Inspired by Hip Hop. Since God & Hip Hop's debut, she has become the Amazon bestselling author of 18 other books and a Licensed & Ordained Evangelist.Ayanna is also the creator of the Write Pray Release book and program designed to equip the masses to self-reflect on past hurt, write it out, and release the pain. Ayanna empowers women to embrace their past stories of triumph and tragedy as the core of their success. She is the creator of God & Hip Hop...a proprietary system that has produced 46 cohort Amazon International Best-Selling Authors. Writers who, like her, were once afraid to share their stories due to shame.Through her company, Thanx A Mills, LLC, Ayanna has delivered numerous literary and empowerment speeches and helped over 150 authors to achieve their Best-Selling dreams through writing, marketing and publishing. Her work is rooted in seeing the power in turning what was designed to destroy you into something that propels you.Ayanna is a native of New York but a current resident of Georgia. She is a happy wife and mom to three sons. She can be reached at the below.

Tell us about you you and your brand as an author and who is your target audience?

I am Ayanna Mills Ambrose, a 18x bestselling Author, Bestselling Book Coach, and Literary Strategist Maximizing Success. My books are bestselling in the US, UK, France, India & Europe.

My books are targeting high performing women who have overcome trauma, and aspiring authors. My books are non fiction transformational books & how to books for aspiring and new authors.

Are you traditional published or self-published? Which do you prefer?

I am self-published. I am also a Self Publishing Consultant for aspiring authors.

What does authorprenurship mean to you and why did you step into this arena?

Authorpreneurship is the best thing. Its when you sell a transform in various forms that's inclusive of books, courses, coaching, speaking and more. I decided to step into this arena because there was a need. Writing is my passion so I write books on writing. However, the authorpreneurship comes in because once they write, then they need help with selling, publishing and overcoming fear to share their messages.

What or who has been your greatest influence in publishing and why?

I created, Write Pray & Release book and program designed to equip the masses to self-reflect on past hurt, write it out, and release the pain. I am inspired by watching women embrace their past stories of triumph and tragedy as the core of their success. Writers who, like me, were once afraid to share their stories due to shame.

What would you say is your greatest win has been as an author CEO?

My greatest win would be my own personal freedom that I've experienced. In addition, I produced 46 (and counting) cohort Amazon International Best Selling Authors and helped over 150 authors to achieve their Best Selling dreams through marketing and/or publishing.

What's the best advice you have received in the publishing arena that you wish to pass on to our readers and those who want to:

When you are writing a book, it may never fill complete, but you must surrender it.

What has been the most effective marketing initiatives or programs you have used to promote your book?

Not being afraid to market to people that I already know. Most are afraid so they start marketing online and with paid ads. People buy from those they know, like and trust, so I always start there.

Do you have any new book or literary projects coming up (or have you just completed a big project ~ reached a milestone, etc.)? If so, please tell us about it.

Yes! My latest anthology, Radical Woman: 1 in a Million & How To Build A 6-Figure Book Business.

Who are you behind the book? Tell us who you are when no one is looking. What do you do for fun/relaxation? What's your favorite vacation spot to unwind?

Happily married wife of less than a year to a rekindled love with my high school sweetheart. My favorite thing is spending time with my husband and our amazing 3 sons. My favorite vacation is anywhere with a beach. I am obsessed with moon & sky gazing.

What's at the top of your list of Goals you plan to accomplish over the next year.

Next year's goal is more self care, more family time, and selling more courses. I am beefing up my program to help authors reach 6-Figures.

What's the best way for our readers to connect with you (feel free to include the links to your social networks and website.

https://linktr.ee/thanxamills

Bestsellingbook.info

https://www.facebook.com/ThanxAMills

https://www.instagram.com/ThanxAMills/

Ceo@thanxamills.com

TOP BLACK AUTHOR OF 2021

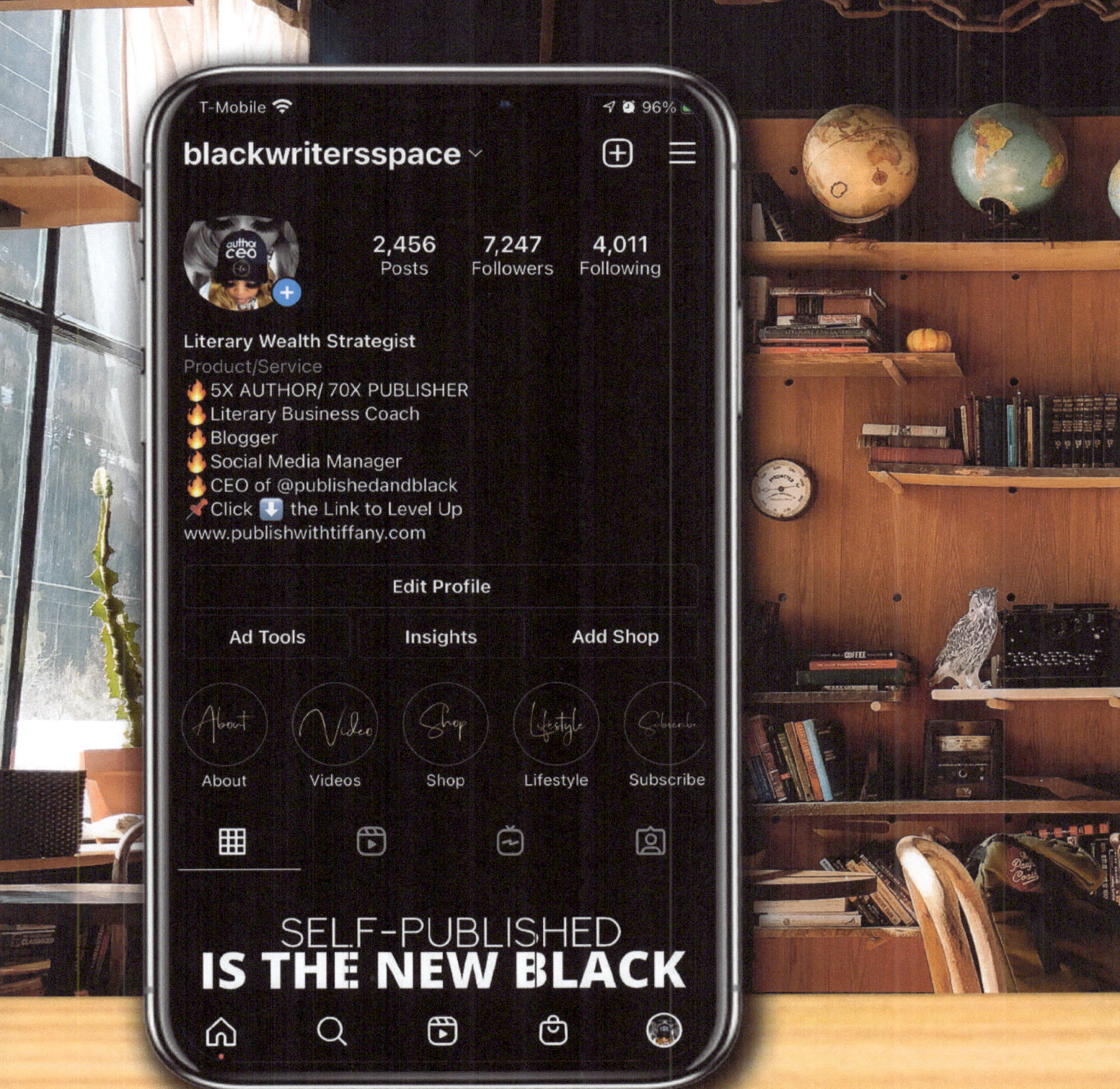

WHAT IS YOUR FAVORITE PLACE TO WRITE ?

I always prefer a nice, quiet place, maybe with my headphones and my favorite smoothie drink or tea. The average would probable prefer coffee. Oops, I'm not a coffee drinker. My belief is that no one can dictate what works for you when writing. No one can see the vision in your head that way you do. Starbucks has absolutely given us options to work in a creative space. Panera Bread is one of my favorite places to write. Not to mention, the food is really great as well. As an author , having the right enviroment to write in is key in producing great content in whatever you are writing.

WWW.PUBLISHEDANDBLACKMAGAZINE.COM

authors . books. film. industry news

AUTHOR DAWN FRANCIS

Author Dawn Francis

bio.

Ms. Francis continues to enhance and inspire others as a vocal trainer, choral director, worship leader and an opera/musical theater actress with her powerful Spinto Soprano voice. In addition, she faithfully served as the Director of the Music Ministry at several churches; zestfully working to fulfill her purpose and destiny, catapulting ministries and musicians to the next level of excellence in the Kingdom of God.. Expanding her roles in multiple pathways - as a Performer, Author, Educator and Visionary; Dawn embodies her calling to help others achieve their full potential and unharness the Strength within.

Ms. Francis is now an author of 2 books on is a bestseller with this collaboration being her third book. She is passionate about sharing and encouraging all

TOP BLACK AUTHOR OF 2021

Who are you behind the book?

I am a wife, aunt, Godmother, sister, minister, psalmist, friend and teacher. I am married to a wonderful man, Leon Francis. I am a mother to many because I am a teacher and educator. I consider myself the favorite aunt and sister. I grew up in a large family. I am the youngest of 8 and I love that. I appreciate every one of my siblings, they are so special.

Tell us who you are when no one is looking.

I am that driven person who always has something going. My nieces say I wake up with rollerskates on (LOL). I love to keep it moving, be it working on projects or helping someone in need. I believe in walking in my purpose and making the most of every moment. My dad used to say, "I don't have time to be tired, I have work to do." I feel that way often but I also know that self care is key.

What do you do for fun/relaxation?

I love reading a good book when I have the time. I like to travel. Music is my other passion, so singing, performing, teaching and training vocalists.

What's your favorite vacation spot to unwind?

I don't think I know my favorite spot yet. I love the islands, that is where my family is from "The Bahamas" so I have to love the Bahamas but my husband is from Jamaica so I love Jamaica too, it's beautiful. But I would say I have a lot more traveling to do before I pick my absolute favorite.

What's at the top of your list of Goals you plan to accomplish over the next year.

To push and complete more projects successfully. We have a Discovering Strength conference coming up in 2022, which is so exciting. We are working on it now and it will be amazing. Other than that, I would say continuing to grow the Discovering Strength Series and release new projects.

Is there anything else you'd like to share with our readers?

Yes, please look for an upcoming live talk show that I will be hosting. On www.Ourtv.network. I am so excited and honored to do this book talk show. I would love and appreciate everyone's support so please share.

What's the best way for our readers to connect with you (feel free to include the links to your social networks and website.

www.dawn-francis.com
www.discoveringstrengthseries.com
FB: drwfrancis
Insgram: drwfrancis
Linkedin : drwfrancis
Clubhouse: drwfrancis

Tell us about you and your brand as an author and who is your target audience?

The brand started after I published my first 2 books and was approached by friends, family and even strangers on how they could write and publish their own stories. I'm all about motivating and encouraging others to follow their passion and dreams and so I opened Life Legacy Publishing as a service to other upcoming authors. This will give them the platform to freely create while getting the support needed to potentially become a best selling author. Being able to leave a life legacy and allowing the legacy of my parents to live on through me is something that connects to my heart. Life Legacy Publishing as a brand takes pride in being uplifting, encouraging, positive, creative and motivational! The first selling collaborative book of the Discovering Strength series, has captivated an audience from many walks of life. It was well received by readers across the globe of all ages - both male and female in various ethnic groups. This collaborative project has taken off, bringing in readers who have shared their gratitude as they have been able find a new perspective. A new perspective as seen through the lens of the author allowing them to grow in their own personal experience.

Are you traditionally published or self-published? Which do you prefer?

I would say being self-published however I am not sure which one I prefer because I have only self-published. I started Life Legacy Publishing specifically to help and guide those who want to write. I don't want people to make the same mistakes that I did. I spent way too much money trying to do things the traditional way. I learned a lot of lessons and I am still learning. But I want to share and use my knowledge and experience to help those who want and need to be helped.

What does authorpreneurship mean to you and why did you step into this arena?

I personally feel as though it's a calling. I literally heard the call and I answered. When you have a story or an idea that can help and benefit someone, it should be shared. Whether for entertainment purposes or for self help. All are needed and I think that's another point: there is room for everyone. All of us are different and we all have different gifts, talents and needs. That is what makes each person and message special.

What or who has been your greatest influence in publishing and why?

My greatest influence in publishing would probably have to be every author's book that I have read. Many of whom have gone the traditional route. I love all authors with positive messages. I also appreciate the entertainment of Terry Mcmillon, Tony Morrison, Danielle Steel and countless others.

How has becoming a published author changed your life overall?

I love it, I love helping people and seeing them thrive and be catapulted to the next level. That is what this does if you push yourself and work it.

What would you say is your greatest win has been as an author CEO?

Helping others and creating a legacy that will live on forever!

What's the best advice you have received in the publishing arena that you wish to pass on to our readers and those who want to publish in the future?

Go for it, don't allow anyone to stand or step in your way. Not even yourself.

What has been the most effective marketing initiatives or programs you have used to promote your book?

Making connections with real people, doing videos, going live and working to stay consistent and relevant. Also being present and sharing real truths that people can relate to.

Do you have any new book or literary projects coming up (or have you just completed a big project ~ reached a milestone, etc.)? If so, please tell us about it.

OMG yes! I have an upcoming show that will be starting on television on ROKU. It is a book talk show and I am super excited about it. The links are below. Please share and join us. Also I have a new book being released from the Best Selling Discovering Strength Series called Hidden In Sight: An Educator's Perspective.

AUTHOR
Jenise McNair

bio........

Bio: Jenise is an Entrepreneur, #1 International Best-Selling Author, 2x Best-Selling Author and a Nine-time Marathoner. Jenise has been featured as seen on several news outlets including ABC, NBC, CBS, and FOX. Jenise McNair overcame many disappointments and hardships that tried to prevent her from unleashing her Greatness Within. After years of feeling like she was losing in every area of her life, she recognized that she would only be able to live up to her Full Potential if she was willing to fight for it! Developing a Winning mindset taught Jenise how to leverage her setbacks so she can always take the lead and Win! When she sets goals, no matter how big or small they are, she is always willing to do whatever is necessary to follow through and execute those goals. In "Potential of a Man vs Truth" and "Fighting for Your Full Potential", Jenise offers powerful insight on how to embrace your personal truths, achieve your goals and follow your dreams while facing obstacles. One book helps you heal while the other book shows you how to Win. Jenise McNair is the owner of Free Her Truths, LLC which was created to coach women who are battling with silent trauma and ongoing hardships. Her mission is to help women embrace their personal truths and leverage their setbacks in life by helping them understand that their Truth is their Power. Jenise is truly passionate about Pushing the women in front of her ahead and Pulling the women behind her along. Jenise is a firm believer that "Self Development is the Foundation of your Success"

TOP BLACK AUTHOR OF 2021

Is there anything else you'd like to share with our readers?

When you want something in life, you have to be willing to Fight for it! You have to be courageous enough to walk in your own personal Truth. Most people will count you out before they count you in; but at the end of the day it's on you to Win. Our biggest and most toughest battle in life is the battle within yourself. So everyday it's important to make an effort to just do the work and become the Greatest Version of yourself. I am a firm believer that "Self Development is the Foundation of your Success". Greatness is in each and everyone of us, so make a choice that striving for Greatness will be your only option.

What's the best way for our readers to connect with you (feel free to include the links to your social networks and website?

You can connect with me on Instagram at Woman_of_Strength31, Facebook at Jenise Neecey McNair or on my website at www.JeniseMcNair.com

"WE ARE HONORED TO CELEBRATE YOU"

www.JeniseMcNair.com

published&black
MAGAZINE

Tell us about you, your brand as an author and who is your target audience?

I am a Serial Entrepreneur and mother of Three. I am the owner of "Free Her Truths LLC" and "WINdemic LLC. Each brand is an extension to each one of my books. Free Her Truths is connected to My first book "Potential of a Man vs. Truth". My target audience are Black millennial mothers and women who are battling with ongoing pain from untreated wounds, past or current. My mission is to help them identify the potential that is inside them, heal properly from trauma and be able to walk and embrace their truth. My mission is also to remind mothers that their Dreams still matter even while supporting and sacrificing for their children. WINdemic is connected to my latest book "Fighting For Your Full Potential". My target audience are also Millennials male or female, who are at a place in their life where they are ready for the "Next Big Thing". They have made a positive shift in their life and they want something different. They are ready to fight for their full potential but just need the guidelines to know how to leverage their setbacks in life and win. This book focuses on Winning while the other book focuses on inner Healing.

Are you traditionally published or self-published? Which do you prefer?

I am a self-published author. I prefer self-published only because it allows me to see everything through from the beginning of the process until the end. It also allows you to always be in control and not having to be on anyone else's time. When you feel the time is right, you're able to just Go For It!

What does authorpreneurship mean to you and why did you step into this arena?

Authorpreneurship is special to me because it allowed me to tell my story and inspired other women to overcome and win. I stepped into this area because God put it on my heart to use my story to impact the hearts and lives of others. This type of arena is like no other. Words are very powerful and all it takes is one sentence to change someone's entire life for the better.

What or who has been your greatest influence in publishing and why?

My father Aaron D. McNair has been my greatest influencer in publishing because of his own personal life story. My father has experienced so many life changing events that would've made anyone want to give up; but his thought process and actions towards life only exemplified compassion, kindness and positivity towards others. He's mentioned on several occasions that he should've written a book about his life. He is truly admirable and knowing his story, only motivated me to share mine. To be honest, I shared a significant portion of his life story in my first book. My father was one of God's greatest gifts given to me. I am so honored to be his daughter and I thank him for being such a loving, supportive and selfless Father. Being in his presence alone always makes me want to be a Greater Version of myself.

How has becoming a published author changed your life overall?

Becoming a published author has changed my life for the better overall because it gave me confirmation that inspiring others to overcome is truly a part of my purpose. Being able to be vulnerable and share my story with the world knowing that someone will be impacted in a positive way; causes me to keep pushing forward and becoming the greatest version of myself. Our purpose is connected to someone else's need.

What would you say your greatest win has been as an author CEO?

My greatest win as an author and CEO would have to be becoming a #1 International Best Selling Author. To be so impactful in different countries of the world was just an amazing feeling. Being an International Best Selling Author allows me to reach more people and make a difference in a positive way. We need more positivity in the world so being able to be that for others is a blessing for me.

What's the best advice you have received in the publishing arena that you wish to pass on to our readers and those who want to publish in the future?

Best advice I received was that whatever that is put on your heart to write a book about; it's meant to be shared with the world. It took me almost 6 years to complete my first book. So regardless if it seems impossible to fit in with your schedule, understand some things are just worth making time for. Wanting to write a book never happens by coincidence, I believe it's a part of God's Plan for your life.

What has been the most effective marketing initiatives or programs you have used to promote your book?

Having your books on you at all times. You are the best marketing tool to promote your books. You can't be afraid to put yourself out there. You have to walk in Authority and know that your book will be an asset to people's lives. Word of mouth is also another great marketing tool. Most people tell it how it is when giving their opinion about books they have read. So Great feedback is always a Win.

Do you have any new books or literary projects coming up (or have you just completed a big project ~ reached a milestone, etc.)? If so, please tell us about it.

I'm actually working on creating "Unleash Your Greatness Academy". In the academy I will be offering a program "The 5 Step Formula To Win in Every Aspect of Your Life". Of course a lot of people want to win in life but most don't know how or where to start. This program will guide women to leverage their setbacks in life and truly understand that their Truth is their Power. The Greatness on the inside of them starts with walking in your Truth. Then you start to win when you learn how to leverage your setbacks. So I am extremely excited to kick that off soon.

Who are you behind the book?

Tell us who you are when no one is looking. What do you do for fun/relaxation? What's your favorite vacation spot to unwind? Who am I behind my book? I Am Human (laughing.) I believe It's important to always be your most authentic self. I'm a loving mom of three. I love hanging out with my friends, cracking jokes and having a drink or two. I'm goofy and I'm definitely an adrenaline junkie. One of the things I love to do that helps me download is Run. I train for Marathons every year to keep me physically in shape and mentally grounded. Also, any free time I get to travel the world, I'm usually gone for two weeks at a time. One of my favorite vacation spots was the Maldives. Very relaxing and the scenery was just breathtaking.

What's at the top of your list of Goals you plan to accomplish over the next year?

Getting more exposure and building my brand so that I can impact more lives. So many women feel alone and I just want to be able to reach more women and provide the support they need while trying to overcome obstacles. I want women to look at my life and know that all things are possible to those who believe and are willing to fight.

PUBLISHING SECRETS

I get authors telling me all the time how they wanna be in front of Oprah, but won't go live on social media. Before you get to Oprah how many books have you sold in your own city. You haven't made yourself known as an author on your block, but expect to magically sell millions of books and become a New York Times Bestseller! This makes no sense. *My #1 Secret* is let's normalize doing the work when it comes to self-publishing.

As black authors I think we must finally let go of the support complaints. You support you. How? Going live daily, finding local events to attend and have your books, banner and flyers/business cards. When was the last time you visited your local library and inquired about getting your book on the shelves. *My #2 Secret* is to make sure you have global distribution and your LCCN NUMBER. Don't do the free ISBN NUMBERS, buy your own ISBN AND BARCODE. We cannot be cheap and expect to make money. Make sure your ISBN is listed under your publishing company name.

The publishing secrets are trapped in everything you refused to do when it comes to marketing your book. There are several ways to market your book that cost little money or no money but require you time. What associations are you part of and active in? Facebook, IG, Clubhouse + Twitter are full of folks who don't know you. Get in front of them and introduce yourself. Build relationships 24/7. Who are you and why should I care? Make folks know who you are and what you do.

Posting a book cover and links alone will never generate the books sales you say you want. Showing up is key. Stop being afraid to show up.

My *Secret #3*-Are you building email lists? You see what happened this week when social media was down. Follower and numbers mean numbers mean nothing if you are not able to communicate with them or if you are not engaging daily.

> "BEFORE YOU GET TO OPRAH, HOW MANY BOOKS HAVE YOU SOLD IN YOUR OWN CITY."

published&black

THE POWER OF
SELF-PUBLISHING
WHY IT MATTERS IN OUR COMMUNITY

FOLLOW US ON INSTAGRAM
@BLACKWRITERSSPACE @PUBLISHEDANDBLACK

WWW.PUBLISHWITHTIFFANY.COM

Tell us about you and your brand as an author and who is your target audience?

I am an author, poet and motivational speaker. My brand is Mario Givens enterprises. My target audience is anyone who has an open mind because my poetry is unorthodox.

Are you traditionally published or self-published? Which do you prefer?

I am self published and I love how I have complete ownership in everything I write.

What does authorpreneurship mean to you and why did you step into this arena?

Authorpreneurship means a lot to me because I want others to understand me and my writings. I really was hesitant on stepping into this because I was afraid of failure. My mentor advised me to take my shot and I did.

What or who has been your greatest influence in publishing and why?

My greatest influencer is author and publisher Tiffany A Green-Hood. Her coaching and expertise with her clients and her dedication is phenomenal.

How has becoming a published author changed your life overall?

Being a published author changed my life because I've met a lot of people on my journey and those relationships I have built has been amazing.

What would you say is your greatest win has been as an author CEO?

My greatest win as an author income is that I'm the first person in my family to become a published author.

What's the best advice you have received in the publishing arena that you wish to pass on to our readers and those who want to publish in the future?

Some of the best advice that I can pass on is to tell others don't be afraid to write a book.

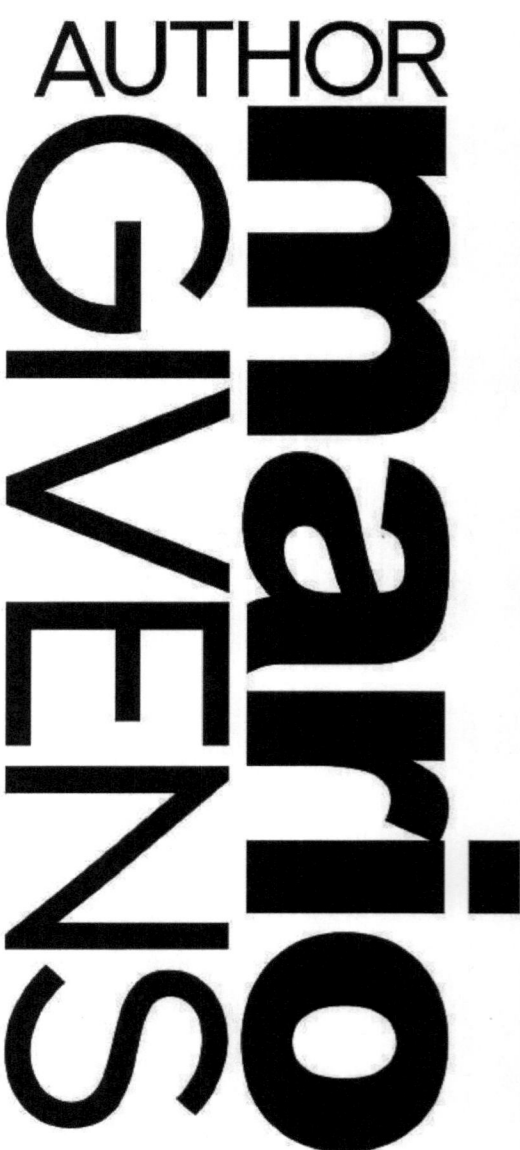

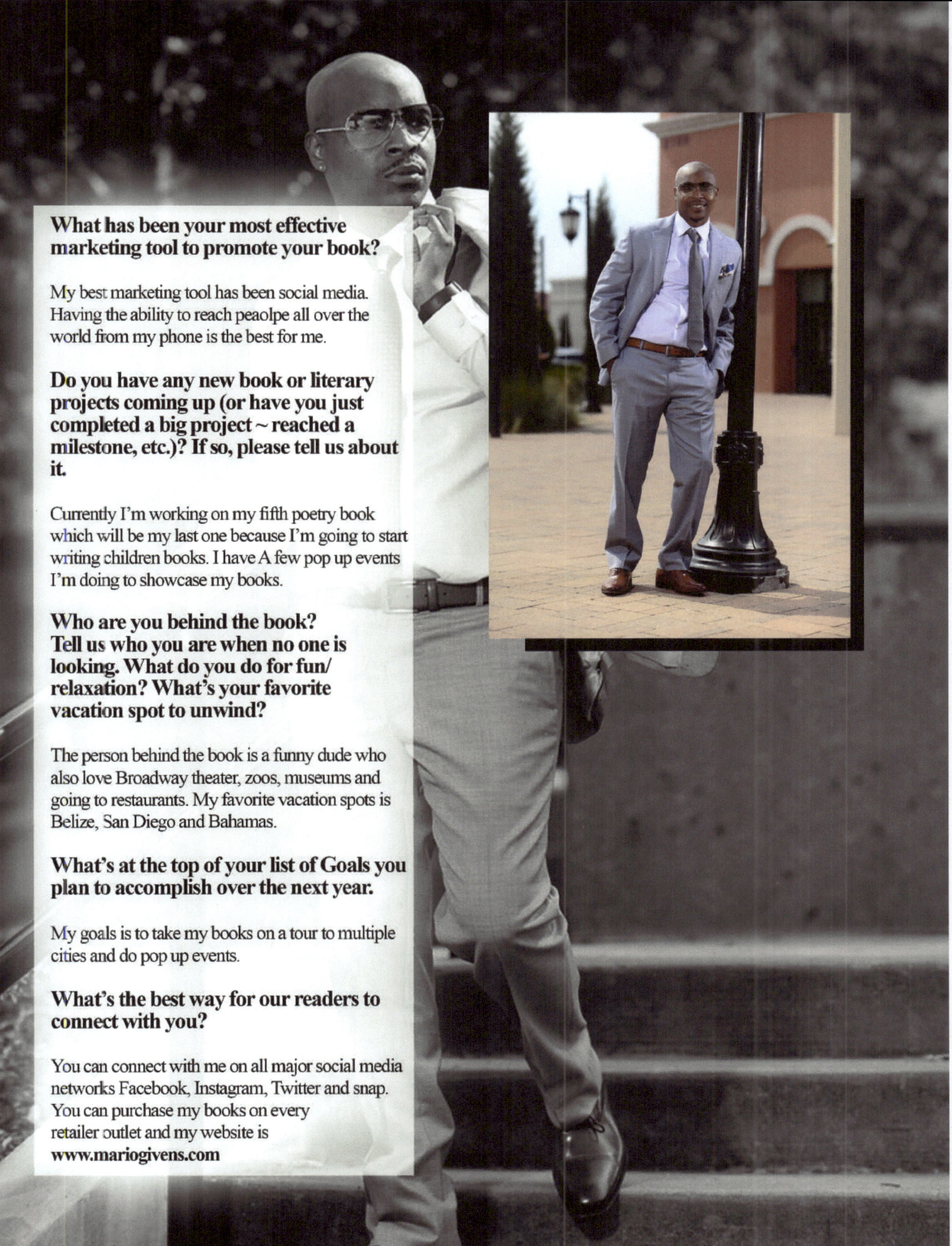

What has been your most effective marketing tool to promote your book?

My best marketing tool has been social media. Having the ability to reach peaolpe all over the world from my phone is the best for me.

Do you have any new book or literary projects coming up (or have you just completed a big project ~ reached a milestone, etc.)? If so, please tell us about it.

Currently I'm working on my fifth poetry book which will be my last one because I'm going to start writing children books. I have A few pop up events I'm doing to showcase my books.

Who are you behind the book? Tell us who you are when no one is looking. What do you do for fun/ relaxation? What's your favorite vacation spot to unwind?

The person behind the book is a funny dude who also love Broadway theater, zoos, museums and going to restaurants. My favorite vacation spots is Belize, San Diego and Bahamas.

What's at the top of your list of Goals you plan to accomplish over the next year.

My goals is to take my books on a tour to multiple cities and do pop up events.

What's the best way for our readers to connect with you?

You can connect with me on all major social media networks Facebook, Instagram, Twitter and snap. You can purchase my books on every retailer outlet and my website is
www.mariogivens.com

CREATE A DOPE BRAND WITH A PLANNER

LEVEL UP WITH PRODUCTS THAT SELL WHILE YOU ARE SLEEP
CREATE A PLANNER TODAY

TAMEDIA +CO.
PUBLISHING | DESIGN | BRANDING | PHOTOGRAPHY

WWW.TAMEDIACO.COM

HOW HAS COVID AFFECTED YOUR BOOK SALES?

> *"The pandemic might not have paid any favors to any other industries, but it has definitely moved the book industry into the limelight."*

Being trapped at home with a limited resource for entertainment drove many people back to their reading roots: parents and children alike, both starving for various literary works. In fact, the pandemic has been extra helpful for brand name authors. Anything that gives the reader more meaning, more emotional attachment turned out to be a win. Publishing companies have even been more receptive to these kinds of authors in leu of the expanding market. Another category of authors that have been on the rise has been diverse background authors, in other words, authors with different ethnicities. Readers took an opportunity such as the pandemic to appreciate different cultures and traditions from around the world.

This congregative action has brought the world close together in difficult times. Events that sparked the Black Lives Matter movement have brought Black talent out into the open. Not only did the world recognize the existence of racism but also working towards eliminating it by supporting numerous black businesses. This, of course, includes black authors and their literary endeavors.

At **Published and Black Magazine**, we provide a scaffold for our self-publishing authors who use their author brand to step into the light. Creating an authentic author brand is what distinguishes many successful authors from struggling ones. In the literary world, the definition of branding varies slightly. It refers to the visual experience before the reader chooses your books. This mainly includes your name, publisher, photography, logos, images, and even typography.

Branding has taken the world by storm ever since advertisement came into market play. Branded cars, shoes, bags, and so on always attract a better quantity of customers by creating a unique aura around their product.

So why should you create this unique aura as an author? A great reason would be to establish a sense of direction. Finalizing your brand name requires you to assess your priorities and values as an author. Once you have successfully measured this goal, you can move on to putting this motivation to carve out your brand name. Something that really says you, and sells you!

At **TA MEDIA CO,** we not only provide the best conten on self-publishing but we also work with you to find yourself and source the right kind of image for your content. Then, we help you capitalize on your existing skills by guiding you to tell your stories to sell. Brand storytelling has become an age-old concept that is most suited for authors and writers like yourself.

Of course, it goes without saying that using your essence to create your brand name will give you an edge over other authors in the market. Your unique edge will attract new readers and keep your old ones loyal too. It is a great way to distinguish yourself from just any generic author.

These are all significant reasons to start contemplating your brand name but be warned. Some authors find it extremely difficult to confront themselves. However, being unsure is only natural at the beginning of your career, which is why an extra push in the right direction is what you need. You will find that at **Published and Black Magazine with Tiffany A. Green-Hood**.

www.publishwithtiffany.com
tamediaco.com

mikayla DIAMOND

TOP BLACK AUTHOR OF 2021

bio~

The world bends at the presence of uniqueness, found at the hems of innovative thought leaders, destined to move culture forward. Embodying this ethic, in unyielding measure; is the dynamic professional, Mikayla Diamond.

Mikayla Diamond is a Best-Selling Author of Patience is Bliss, empowerment coach, speaker, rhapsodist, and multi-preneur, with an increasing passion for the influence, strategic development, and ultimate success, of growing professionals. As the CEO and Founder of Empowering Generations, LLC, as well as Visionary of the 21st Century Woman Club & Network, Mikayla is reputed as one leading with impact; bringing soulful depth, wisdom, and compassion to the marketplace. A while empowering and equipping women entrepreneurs propelled in their purpose, to share their story, skills, spiritual gifts, experience, and expertise by way of increasing visibility, impact, and income, through the vernacular of brand marketing space; via podcasting, e-books, and e-courses.

Her mantra is clear: Mikayla helps entrepreneurial hopefuls recognize that their greatest potential lies within. Displaying a commitment to those in need of exhortation, Mikayla helps clients to envision and achieve infinite success and elevation; along with the profound realization that with her aid, they can rise together.

Mikayla's success is sustained by a sincere regard for the acquisition of knowledge, an estimable work-ethic, and an overwhelming propensity for servitude, and achievement. To date, Mikayla holds more than eight professional certifications; including: Life Coaching, 7 Habits of Highly Effective People, Tax Specialist, Naval Education Physical Readiness, and many more. An accomplished laureate, Mikayla has received a myriad of diverse honors for her creative contribution to the philanthropic, business, and branding world. She was named amongst one of the phenomenal TOP 40 Most Influential Dreamers, Movers & Shakers Column 2020, USN Good Conduct Award in recognition of fidelity, zealous, and obedient service; the Letter of Commendation Award for an outstanding professional performance of duty as USN Hospital Corpsman Veteran, Military Health Center, Director of Branch Clinics; along with demonstrating excellence, at the Naval Medical Center San Diego, in support of ENDURING FREEDOM and IRAQI FREEDOM; an immaculate display of her total dedication to duty, whilst upholding the highest standards, of the United States Service.

Inspired most by successful people who fulfill their God-given dreams, authentic purpose, and passion, Mikayla Diamond contributes her relationship with success, to an undying appreciation for female empowerment. In 2017 and 2018, she organized a 6-month multi-state book tour for the sole intention of energizing women entrepreneurs, to take hold of their influence; in the marketplace, in their purpose, passion, and potential. It is with this distinction, she remains a reputable voice in audiences, worldwide.

When Mikayla is not out showing entrepreneurs how to level-up in their daily lives, she remains an asset to her local communal body, and a loving member of her family and friendship circles.

Mikayla Diamond. Leader. Curator. Enthusiast.

published&black™

Author MIKAYLA **DIAMOND**

1. Tell us about you and your brand as an author and who is your target audience?

I'm best-selling author, business empowerment coach, and speaker who celebrates cultural diversity valuing differences and is dedicated to equipping entrepreneurs to find their passion in life, which translates into your ideal business model to accommodate you in life and business.

My brand's mission is to empower and equip entrepreneurs grow their business in alignment with who they are, what they love to do and how they want to serve in the marketplace.

Your Life's Calling + Your Purpose-Driven Ideal Business = Freedom & Abundance in life and business.

2. Are you traditional published or self-published? Which do you prefer?

I'm a self-published author recognizing some of its benefits with it giving you the opportunity, flexibility, creativity and authority to expand and scale as an entrepreneur, while retaining 100% rights to your work. Also, self-publishing allows you to retain full control over what you're writing about and how you write it. You take charge of book marketing, design and distribution to develop your own unique branding as an author.

In addition, you yield higher royalty rates, which potentially provides more money for marketing than traditional publishing which increases your potential to receive the highest profitable income with an effective marketing plan to sell the same amount of books or more. As a result, providing you a return on investment with opportunities to reach your target market with greater levels of impact.

3. What does authorprenurship mean to you and why did you step into this arena?

As a faith-based authorpreneur, authorpreneurship is defined as authority in your field of excellence. I stepped into this arena to lead with impact. In this arena, you are able to leverage your story, skills, spiritual gifts, expertise and experience in your book(s) as a tool and resource as the foundation to launch a platform for your business, maximizing your book's potential to generate multiple streams of income via coaching, consulting, speaking engagements, podcasting, conferences, book tours, seminars, workshops to bring solutions to your target market.

4. What or who has been your greatest influence in publishing and why?

My greatest influence in publishing has being my relationship with God. The inspiration of Holy Spirit encouraged me with these words,"There is room for your book in heaven's library." It is an eternal legacy lasting from generation to generation. I, myself have read many books from phenomenal authors of 20-40 years of experience that has impacted my life significantly in a short time span of reading their masterpiece. When your book makes a big impact in someone's life, he or she continues to share.

5. How has becoming a published author changed your life overall?

When you publish a book, your message is no longer on a page. It takes on a life of its own. As a published best-selling author, I am a huge advocate for all who desire to become an author. It has been a total game-changer. It was God's trump card of everything He allowed me to experience in over three decades and provided me the freedom of expression to publish my purpose to impact and transform lives to the glory of God. It is a life-long impact and legacy in life and business. It further enabled me to build my credibility, expertise and influence in the marketplace. It is the key that created an infinite door of opportunities with numerous people wanting to learn from me with the motive of taking what I've learned and apply it to their businesses or personal lives.

6. What would you say is your greatest win has been as an author CEO?

My greatest win as a CEO Author is the fact that I have been able to expand and scale my business model through books as part of the foundation of my overall business plan.

7. What's the best advice you have received in the publishing arena that you wish to pass on to our readers and those who want to publish in the future?

There is more money to be made in publishing, in addition to selling your books.

When you get the value you receive from coaching, speaking, consulting, working with clients, and generating leads for yourself or someone else, then you have a solid business model. Get your story, skills, expertise or experience published. The best advice I have received in publishing...be a publisher.

8. What has been the most effective marketing initiatives or programs you have used to promote your book?

My best marketing initiative has been to partner with other experts as a visionary to launch a 6-month multi-state book tour collectively with local state speakers and experts to empower and equip entrepreneurs in life and business. I used social media to book my tour stops and to invite people to attend to not only meet online but in person. This initiative enabled me and my book to be seen and heard with the goal to build the greatest number of relationship with entrepreneurs in life and business to position myself as their trusted entrepreneurial authority and expert being a professional coach and speaker.

9. Do you have any new book or literary projects coming up (or have you just completed a big project ~ reached a milestone, etc.)? If so, please tell us about it.

My newest project is my new business launch utilizing my books as the foundation of the curriculum in my coaching practice to serve my clients in the 21st Century Woman Signature Coaching Program. My business coaching program is an extension of my books and expounds on my signature methodology that I teach in all of my courses and empowerment sessions. The program has been designed to serve the needs of the modern woman who is looking for a path forward to create more time, money, relationships, joy and contribution.

10. Who are you behind the book? Tell us who you are when no one is looking. What do you do for fun/relaxation? What's your favorite vacation spot to unwind?

I am the delighted mother of three who loves going to amusement parks with the kids, especially water parks, as well as go-kart driving and playing arcade games with them. In my own personal free time, I love traveling, sharing my poetic expressions at poetry events. Enjoy seeing sunsets at the beach, vibing to music, and enjoy eating out with friends and family. One of my favorite places of relaxation for staycation to unwind is Red Rock Resort & Spa.

11. What's at the top of your list of Goals you plan to accomplish over the next year.

Connect & Collaborate With 100 Entrepreneurs Over the Next Year: My goal is to connect with entrepreneurs over the next year. I would like to build a team network of 100 entrepreneurial minds who are ready to launch, scale, and expand their business as a collaborative effort.

12. Is there anything else you'd like to share with our readers?

Connect with people who are interested in what you have to offer. This is the perfect place to do so. I'm looking forward to growing with you. Let's do that by staying in constant contact. This way, I can send you relevant, timely information to help you run your business better and grow your profits.

13. What's the best way for our readers to connect with you (feel free to include the links to your social networks and website.

Let's stay connected. Below is the best way to contact me.

Website: https://www.mikayladiamond.com
Instagram: @iammikayladiamond
Clubhouse: @iammikayladiamond
Facebook: @iammikayladiamond
Email: admin@mikayladiamond.com
Contact number: 909.375.8361

DIAMOND

WWW.TIFFANYSPEAKSREAL.COM

TIFFANY SPEAKS REAL
PODCAST
BUSINESS. PUBLISHING. MEDIA

WITH TIFFANY A GREEN-HOOD

EVERYWHERE PODCASTS ARE STREAMING

INTRODUCING, AUTHOR, PUBLISHER, ENTREPRENEUR TIFFANY A. GREEN-HOOD BRINGING INNOVATIVE, LIFE-CHANGING, INFORMATION AND CONVERSATIONS ABOUT LIFE, BUSINESS AND PUBLISHING. BEING FLUENT IN PHOTOGRAPHY, PUBLISHING, BUSINESS, AND SOCIAL **MEDIA, TIFFANY HAS GAINED LOTS OF DO'S AND DON'TS IN BUSINESS AND ENTREPRENEURSHIP. ARE YOU READY TO BREAK BARRIERS OFF OF YOUR BLOODLINE THAT HAVE HELD YOU BACK? ARE YOU READY TO TRULY MAKE YOUR DREAMS COME TRUE? AND FOR THOSE IN THE BACK, YES YOU, NO MORE PEOPLE-PLEASING. TUNE IN WEEKLY FOR TRANSFORMATIONAL MESSAGES TO CHANGE YOUR LIFE, BUSINESS, AND BRAND.**

SELF-PUBLISHED IS THE NEW BLACK

I STARTED MY PUBLISHING COMPANY WITH ZERO BUDGET. I READ, RESEARCHED AND TOOK NOTES ON FREE WEBINARS. I STARTED GOING LIVE ON PERISCOPE WITH ZERO FOLLOWERS. THE REST IS HISTORY

published**&black** MAGAZINE

THE
Literary Wealth Strategist

TIFFANY A GREEN-HOOD

GET FEATURED IN OUR NOVEMBER ISSUE

EDITOR@PUBLISHEDANDBLACK.COM

published&black
MAGAZINE

www.ingramcontent.com/pod-product-compliance
Lightning Source LLC
Chambersburg PA
CBHW041059070526
44579CB00002B/12